FOCUS ON

ANCIENT EGYPTIANS

ANITA GANERI

GLOUCESTER PRESS
London · New York · Sydney

© Aladdin Books Ltd 1993

All rights reserved

Designed and produced by
Aladdin Books Ltd
28 Percy Street
London W1P 9FF

First published in
Great Britain in 1993 by
Watts Books
96 Leonard Street
London EC2A 4RH

ISBN 0 7496 1077 8

A CIP catalogue record for this book is
available from the British Library.

Printed in Belgium

Design	David West Children's Book Design
Designer	Flick Killerby
Series Director	Bibby Whittaker
Editor	Fiona Robertson
Picture research	Emma Krikler
Illustrators	Sergio Momo
	David Burroughs
	David Russell

The author, Anita Ganeri (M.A.Cantab),
has written numerous books for children
on history, natural history and other topics.

The educational and historical
consultant, Dr Anne Millard, works
for the extra-mural department of
London University. She has written
many books for children on history
and archaeology.

INTRODUCTION

The Ancient Egyptian civilisation was one of the oldest and greatest in the world. Egyptian learning, Egyptian architecture and even Egyptian gods can all be detected in later civilisations, such as those of Greece and Rome. The modern fascination with Ancient Egypt began in the 18th century. Since then, countless tombs and temples have been excavated, and wonderful treasures uncovered. This book aims to give an insight into the splendour of Ancient Egypt and the lives of the Ancient Egyptians, and includes information about language and literature, science and maths, history, geography and the arts. The key below shows how the subjects are divided up.

Geography

The symbol of the planet Earth shows where geographical facts and activities are included. These sections look at the mineral resources of Ancient Egypt, and at the importance of trade with countries such as Nubia.

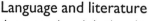

Language and literature

An open book is the sign for activities which involve language. These explore some of the numerous myths and legends in Ancient Egypt surrounding death and the afterlife. They also look at the effect of Egyptian culture on contemporary writers.

Science and maths

The microscope symbol shows where a science or maths subject is included. Mummification is perhaps the best known scientific process used by the Ancient Egyptians. Also discussed are the beliefs surrounding sacred animals.

History

The sign of the scroll and hourglass indicates where historical information is given. These sections look at events in Ancient Egyptian history, and examine the impact of Egyptian culture on our society today.

Social history

The symbol of the family shows where information about social history is given. These sections aim to provide an insight into the everyday lives of the Ancient Egyptians. Topics covered include the role of women, what the Egyptians wore and what they ate.

Arts, crafts and music

The symbol showing a sheet of music and art tools signals where information on arts, crafts or music are included. Activities involve writing out a message using Ancient Egyptian hieroglyphs. These sections also look at the different influences on Egyptian art.

CONTENTS

THE LAND OF EGYPT 4/5

THE OLD KINGDOM 6/7

THE PYRAMID COMPLEX................8/9

THE MIDDLE KINGDOM 10/11

LANGUAGE AND WRITING..........12/13

THE NEW KINGDOM 14/15

THE GODS OF EGYPT 16/17

SOCIAL STRUCTURE 18/19

THE FARMER'S YEAR...................20/21

EGYPTIANS AT HOME 22/23

BURIAL CUSTOMS.......................24/25

FOREIGN PHARAOHS 26/27

THE EGYPTIAN LEGACY..............28/29

DATE CHART.............................30/31

GLOSSARY 31

INDEX...32

THE LAND OF EGYPT

More than 7,000 years ago, one of the world's first and greatest civilisations grew up along the banks of the River Nile in Egypt. The earliest villages were settled by hunters driven east from the drought-stricken grasslands of central Africa. In time, the villages formed two kingdoms – Lower Egypt in the Nile Delta and Upper Egypt in the valley. In about 3100 BC, King Menes united the country and built his capital at Memphis. He also established the first Egyptian Dynasty (a line of kings from the same family), known as Dynasty I. Over the next 2,000 years, Ancient Egypt was to grow and flourish.

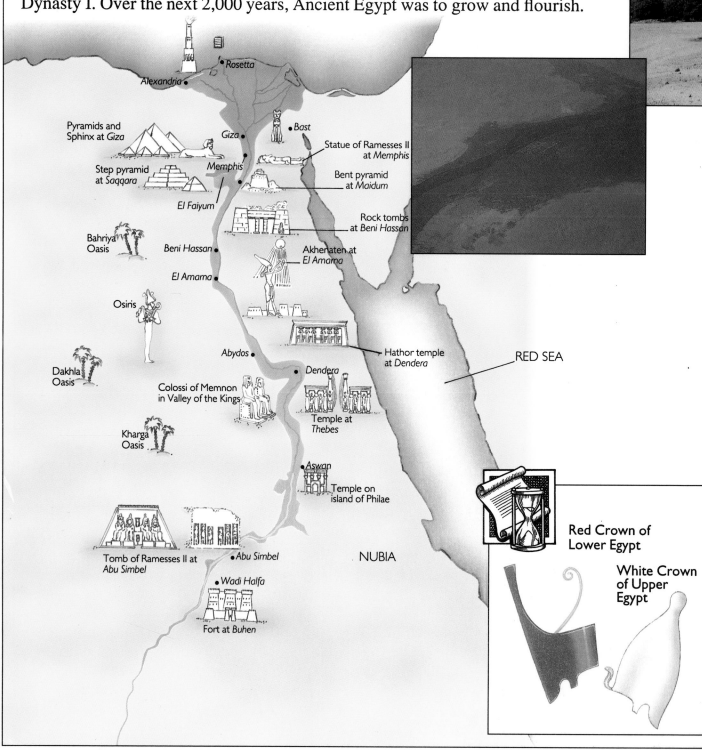

Rosetta

Alexandria

Pyramids and Sphinx at *Giza*

Giza

Bast

Statue of Ramesses II at *Memphis*

Memphis

Step pyramid at *Saqqara*

Bent pyramid at *Maidum*

El Faiyum

Bahriya Oasis

Rock tombs at *Beni Hassan*

Beni Hassan

Akhenaten at *El Amarna*

El Amarna

Osiris

Dakhla Oasis

Abydos

Dendera

Hathor temple at *Dendera*

RED SEA

Colossi of Memnon in Valley of the Kings

Temple at *Thebes*

Kharga Oasis

Aswan

Temple on island of Philae

Tomb of Ramesses II at *Abu Simbel*

Abu Simbel

NUBIA

Wadi Halfa

Fort at Buhen

Red Crown of Lower Egypt

White Crown of Upper Egypt

The desert

For the Ancient Egyptians, the Red Land, or desert, that lay to the east and west of their country (see photos, left) was a dangerous and sinister place. The area was largely uncultivated and desolate, with just a few fertile spots, called oases, where underground water seeped to the surface. Some of the more isolated oases in the Western desert were used as places of banishment for political and other prisoners.

The Inundation

The Greek historian, Herodotus, described Ancient Egypt as the "Gift of the Nile". Each year, the Nile flooded and deposited fertile, black soil on both banks. The time of flooding was known as the Inundation. It was caused by melting snow and rainwater from the mountains in Ethiopia swelling the river. This extra water reached Egypt in June or July. When the flooding began to subside in October, the soil was ideal for farming. The Ancient Egyptians called the fertile area Kemet, which means "Black Land". The surrounding desert was called Deshret, or "Red Land". The Nile also provided water for irrigation and was Ancient Egypt's main transport route.

Natural resources

The rich black, silty soil of the Nile was Ancient Egypt's greatest natural resource, but not its only one. Large amounts of limestone, sandstone and granite were quarried from the desert hills above the Nile, and used for building and sculpture. The deserts also contained rich supplies of gold, copper and semi-precious stones, such as amethysts, garnets and felspars. Dry river beds, called wadis, were used as trade routes across the desert to the coast of the Red Sea.

Granite statue of Ramesses II

Double Crown of the united Egypt

King Menes

When King Menes united Egypt, he took the official title of "King of Upper and Lower Egypt". The two royal crowns – the White of Upper Egypt and the Red of Lower Egypt – were combined at this time to form the Double Crown.

A colourful legacy

Egyptian culture is still represented in musicals like *Joseph and his Amazing Technicolour Dreamcoat*. The tale is based on a Bible story about a boy who was sold into slavery in Egypt. Joseph helped to save Egypt from famine by advising the Pharaoh to store extra grain.

THE OLD KINGDOM

The Old Kingdom began in about 2686 BC with Dynasty III. This was one of the greatest periods in Egyptian history. The country was ruled by a strong central government, and extended its trading links with Nubia and with the lands around the Red Sea and the Mediterranean. Art, culture and scholarship also flourished. The Old Kingdom was the great age of pyramid building (see pages 8/9). After the death of King Pepi II in 2152 BC, however, a period of chaos followed, known as the First Intermediate Period.

Date chart

c.5000-3100 BC Predynastic Period
c.3100 BC King Menes unites Egypt

c.3100-2686 BC Archaic Period (Dynasties I and II)
c.2686-2150 BC The Old Kingdom (Dynasties III and IV)
c.2686-2613 BC Reign of King Zoser (Dynasty III)
c.2589-2566 BC Reign of King Khufu (Cheops) (Dynasty IV)
c. 2580 BC Building of the Great Pyramid of Cheops at Giza
c.2494-2345 BC Dynasty V. Kings devoted to the sun god, Re, and take the title "Son of Re".
c. 2246-2150 BC Reign of King Pepi II (Dynasty VI). The longest recorded reign in history.
c.2150-2040 BC First Intermediate Period (Dynasties VIII–X)

LOWER EGYPT

Giza
Saqqara — Memphis

Hierakonopolis

Abydos

UPPER EGYPT

Aswan

1st Cataract

TRADE AND RAIDS

NUBIA

2nd Cataract

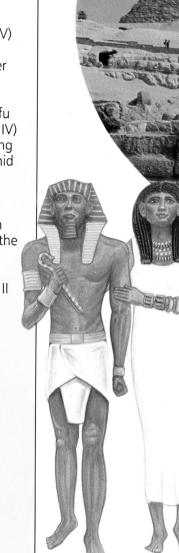

King Menkaure and his queen

Ancient Egypt was ruled by Kings who were believed to be the god, Horus, in human form. From about 1554 BC, the King was also called Pharaoh, from the Egyptian words "per aa", meaning "great house". The position of King was inherited, and passed to the eldest son of the King's chief wife. In an effort to keep the royal blood pure, the King often married a close relation, such as his sister or half-sister.

The administration

The King appointed officials called viziers to help him rule. The viziers acted for the King in all matters of government and the administration of justice. Ancient Egypt was divided into 42 administrative districts, called nomes. Each nome was governed on behalf of the King by an official called a nomarch.

Taxes in Ancient Egypt were paid according to an individual's profession. Thus, farmers paid their taxes in crops, while skilled workers were taxed on the goods or services they produced. A special labour tax called a corvée provided troops and government workers.

Actual boats have been found in a number of the tombs around the pyramids at Giza. They were probably used by the King in life, and to carry him to his final resting place. The boat shown right belonged to King Khufu. It can be seen today at Giza.

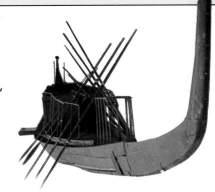

The Sphinx

The three great pyramids at Giza (left) were built about 4,500 years ago, during the Old Kingdom, as tombs for the Kings, Khufu, Khafre and Menkaure. The pyramids are guarded by a huge stone statue, called a sphinx. It has the body of a lion and a human head whose features are thought to be those of King Khafre. Khafre succeeded Khufu after the short reign of Khufu's son, Ra'djedef, who was seen as a usurper.

King Ra'djedef (above left) followed his father, King Khufu, to the throne.

Trade with Nubia

The country of Nubia lay to the south of Egypt. It was considered so important for trade that the Egyptians cut a canal through the First Cataract (a place where rocks blocked the River Nile – see map, left) to speed up the journey to Nubia. The Egyptians bought leopard skins, ivory, ebony, slaves and later gold from Nubia in exchange for luxury goods.

The illustration (right) shows some of the goods that came from Nubia: rings of gold, ebony, panther-skins and apes.

THE PYRAMID COMPLEX

The Great Pyramid of Giza, built for King Khufu, was one of the Seven Wonders of the ancient world. The pyramids are still amongst the greatest engineering feats ever known. They were built as permanent tombs for the Kings, where they and the goods they were taking into the next world would be safe from thieves (see pages 24/25). The first pyramids had stepped sides so that the King's soul could climb up them to reach heaven. They were later built with straight sides to represent the Sun's rays. The King could walk up the rays to the Sun god.

Stone quarries

Vast amounts of stone were needed to build the pyramids. The Great Pyramid alone contains about 2,300,000 stone blocks, each weighing up to two and a half tonnes. Stone from quarries nearby was hauled to the site on sledges. Limestone from Tura and granite from Aswan were brought down the Nile by barge.

The King's body was brought by river in a highly decorated funerary barge. It was prepared for burial in the Valley Temple on the bank of the river, then carried down a long, covered causeway (corridor) to the Mortuary Temple. Here prayers were said for the King's soul before his body was taken into the burial chamber.

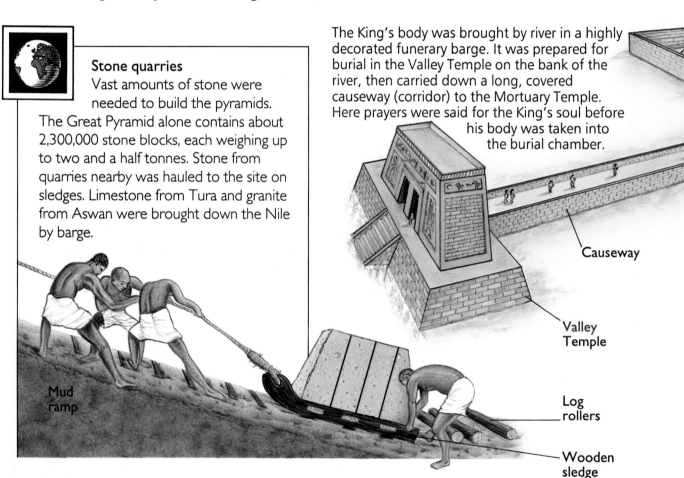

Causeway

Valley Temple

Mud ramp

Log rollers

Wooden sledge

Measuring

The pyramids required a great deal of planning. Firstly, the base was marked out to form a perfect square. Step-like terraces were then built, onto which stone blocks were later laid. The Egyptian methods were so accurate that experts using modern equipment have found the south-east corner of the Great Pyramid is only 1cm higher than the north-east corner.

The accuracy of pyramid angles may have been achieved by counting the revolutions of a rolling drum (left).

Water trenches, measuring rods and string were used to make sure the pyramids's foundations were level(right).

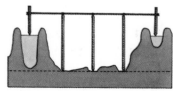

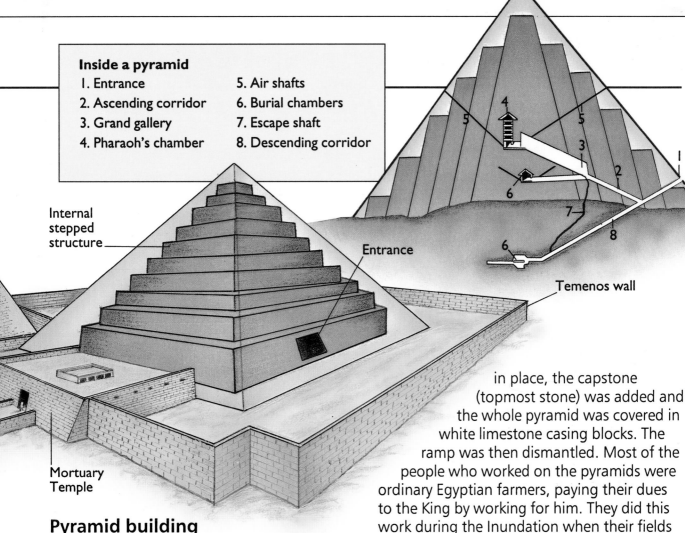

Inside a pyramid
1. Entrance
2. Ascending corridor
3. Grand gallery
4. Pharaoh's chamber
5. Air shafts
6. Burial chambers
7. Escape shaft
8. Descending corridor

Internal stepped structure

Entrance

Temenos wall

Mortuary Temple

Pyramid building

The Ancient Egyptians had no cranes, trucks or mechanised building equipment. Teams of workers dragged the huge stone blocks into position using wooden sledges which they hauled up a mud and brick ramp. The ramp was made higher and longer as the pyramid grew, layer by layer. When all the layers were in place, the capstone (topmost stone) was added and the whole pyramid was covered in white limestone casing blocks. The ramp was then dismantled. Most of the people who worked on the pyramids were ordinary Egyptian farmers, paying their dues to the King by working for him. They did this work during the Inundation when their fields were flooded.

The one that went wrong
The core of the Maidum Pyramid (below) rises up from a pile of debris. It is all that remains of an early failed attempt at a true pyramid. The pyramid was begun at the end of Dynasty III, and was originally a seven-stepped structure. An eighth step was later added, along with a limestone casing to give a smooth finish. However, the pyramid had no proper foundations and as a result, it collapsed.

Mexican pyramids
In the 13th to 15th centuries AD, the Aztecs of Mexico built their own pyramids. Temples to their sun god were built on top. A stairway at the front of the pyramid enabled priests to climb up to the temple and offer sacrifices. Amazingly, the Aztecs had never seen, or even heard of, the Egyptian pyramids.

A Mexican pyramid

THE MIDDLE KINGDOM

The Middle Kingdom began in about 2040 BC when King Mentuhotep II of Dynasty XI reunited Egypt. About 1991 BC, a vizier, Amenemhat, seized the throne. Under his rule and that of his heirs (Dynasty XII), Egypt became wealthy and powerful again. However, a series of weak rulers followed in Dynasty XIII and by about 1670 BC, Egypt was overrun by the Hyksos people from Asia. In about 1640 BC, the Second Intermediate Period, one of the darkest periods in Egypt's history, began.

Date chart

c.2040-1640 BC
The Middle Kingdom
c.2040 BC
Mentuhotep II overthrows his rivals

and reunites Egypt under Dynasty XI
c.1991-1783 BC
Under the Dynasty XII Kings, Egypt conquers Nubia and builds a string of forts on the Second Cataract

c.1991-1962 BC
Reign of Amenemhat I (Dynasty XII)
c. 1787-1783 BC
Reign of Princess Sobek-neferu as "King" (Dynasty XII)
c.1786-1640 BC
Dynasty XIII
c.1670 BC Hyksos overrun Egypt
c.1640-1552 BC
The Second Intermediate Period

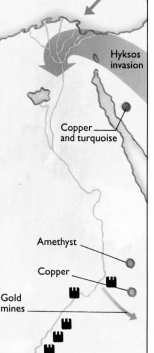

Cedar wood trade

Hyksos invasion

Copper and turquoise

Amethyst

Copper

Gold mines

KEY

O Mines

⬛ Forts

During the Middle Kingdom, the Egyptians conquered Nubia and traded far and wide. Egyptian traders brought rare and valuable goods to Egypt, and increased their country's wealth and power. They brought gold from the Nubian desert (below) and cedar and cypress wood from Syria and Lebanon. The merchants did not use money – they bartered with other goods, or with copper weights, called *deben*.

Art by design

Egyptian works of art were governed by strict rules. The artists first applied a layer of plaster to the wall to make it level. Then they marked out a grid to help them get the drawings in proportion. Their sketches were corrected by a supervisor, then they filled in details and colour. Important people, such as pharaohs, were represented by large figures, unimportant people by little ones. Perspective followed traditional guidelines, and was not used realistically. Figures were usually drawn in profile, with a full-view eye.

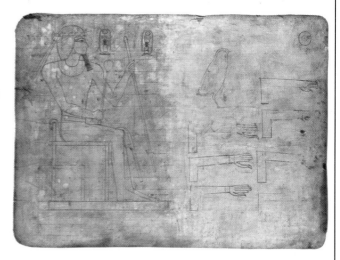

The engraving left, shows a procession of armed attendants. Each Egyptian had a shield decorated with an individual design. This enabled him to recognise his own shield instantly when called to battle. Military equipment was often included in tombs as a symbol of protection in the afterworld.

Egyptian soldiers used spears, axes, swords, bows and arrows and maces, usually made of wood and bronze. They carried ox-hide shields. From the New Kingdom onwards, they wore armour made out of leather strips.

Chariot charge

The Hyksos army used horse-drawn chariots and improved bows to help them defeat the Egyptians. These had never been seen in Egypt before. By the time of the New Kingdom, they had become an important part of the Egyptian army which, having learnt to use the chariots and weapons of their enemies, succeeded in driving the invaders out. The Pharaoh himself became Commander-in-Chief. The army divisions were named after gods, such as Amun and Re.

A New Kingdom chariot

LANGUAGE AND WRITING

The Ancient Egyptians spoke a language related to the languages of the Middle East and North Africa. Those who could, wrote using a system of picture writing, called hieroglyphics. The Egyptians began using hieroglyphics in about 3000 BC, shortly after the first known examples of writing appeared in Sumer (now south eastern Iraq).

Each picture, or hieroglyph, could stand for an object and a sound. Some represented one letter; others up to five letters. These were always consonants. Vowels were not written down.

Ink blocks

Reed pens

A scribe

Breaking the code

Hieroglyphics were last used in about AD 394. For more than 1,400 years no one could read or understand them. In 1799, however, a soldier in Napoléon Bonaparte's army in Egypt found a large, stone slab – the Rosetta Stone. On the stone was a text carved by Egyptian priests in 196 BC to mark the crowning of King Ptolemy V. The same text was written out in Ancient Egyptian hieroglyphs, demotic script (a simpler form of hieroglyphs) and Greek. By comparing the three, a French scholar called Jean François Champollion, was finally able to crack the code in 1822.

Champollion

The Rosetta Stone

Writing hieroglyphs

The word "hieroglyph" is Greek for sacred carvings. Egyptian hieroglyphs were usually written or carved by highly trained men called scribes. Egyptian society was based on keeping records, and scribes were therefore very important. Many rose to positions of great authority because they could read and write. Use the symbols below to write your own hieroglyphic message.

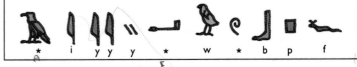

Papyrus paper

The Egyptians wrote on a paper-like material, called papyrus, made of reeds. The pith was taken out of the reeds and cut into strips. These were laid flat in layers, covered in cloth and pounded with heavy stones or a mallet to weld them together. The papyrus was then polished to give a smooth, flat surface. Sheets of papyrus were often fixed together to form a roll.

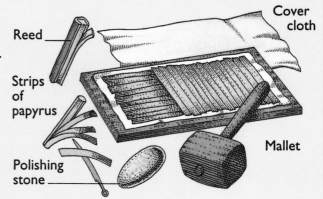

Reed

Cover cloth

Strips of papyrus

Polishing stone

Mallet

For daily use, two simpler, less formal shorthand scripts were created. Hieratic script (left) was used in the Old Kingdom. By about 700 BC, demotic (from the Greek word *demotikos*, meaning "popular") script was in use.

Hieroglyphs (above) were not used in everyday life. They were reserved for important inscriptions, such as those on tombs and temples and for affairs of state.

B

There were many different ways of writing hieroglyphs. They could be written from left to right, right to left or top to bottom. If an animal faced right (A), you read from right to left. If it faced left (B), you read from left to right.

A

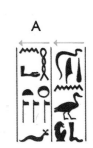

A

B

*No translation

The name or symbol of a ruler appeared in hieroglyphs within an oval frame called a cartouche (shown left).

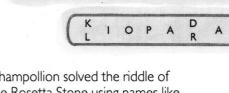

K I O P A D A
L O R

P O L Y S
T O M S

Champollion solved the riddle of the Rosetta Stone using names like Ptolemy and Cleopatra (left and above). See if you can spot which letters appear in both names.

m   n   r   h   h   ch   h (soft)   s   s   sh   q   k   g (hard)   t   tj   d   dj

THE NEW KINGDOM

The New Kingdom began in about 1552 BC and saw Egypt build up a huge empire. The Hyksos were driven out and the Pharaoh himself took command of the army. By the time of Tuthmosis III (c. 1479-1425 BC), Egypt had become the greatest power in the whole Middle East. The kings of Dynasty XIX included Ramesses II, a great soldier and builder of temples. During the reign of Ramesses III, Egypt was attacked by a group of raiders called the Sea Peoples (see below). Although they were defeated, Egypt never fully recovered.

At least two queens seized the throne of Egypt during the New Kingdom. The greatest was Queen Hatshepsut (1473-1458 BC). She married her half-brother, Tuthmosis II. When he died, she acted first as regent to his heir and successor, the boy Tuthmosis III, then as "King". She was always addressed as "His Majesty". One of Hatshepsut's greatest achievements was to send a fleet of ships to the land of Punt, a mysterious land on the east coast of Africa. No one from Egypt had been there for over 200 years. The expedition brought back myrrh for making the incense used in temples.

Hatshepsut

Ramesses II in his Blue or War Crown

Boat building
Boats were the main form of transport in Ancient Egypt. The earliest types were made of reeds, and were rowed. Sails were soon invented and wood gradually replaced reeds as the main building material. Boats were used mostly for trade at home and abroad, transport and funerals. When the Sea Peoples from the north-east Mediterranean invaded Egypt, Ramesses III was forced to use a fleet of warships to fight them.

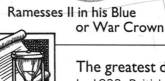

A trading ship

The greatest discovery
In 1922, British archaeologist, Howard Carter, discovered the tomb of King Tutankhamun in the Valley of the Kings. The tomb was the only royal tomb of the New Kingdom to be found intact, and was full of wonderful treasures – gold jewellery, statues, furniture, clothes. The greatest find of all was the mummy of the Pharaoh himself, his face covered by an exquisite gold death mask (right).

The temple of Amun-Re at Karnak was enlarged and extended by Ramesses II. He added a great pillared hypostyle, or hall, of 134 painted columns (see below). The finished temple was big enough to hold several cathedrals. Ramesses also built a spectacular rock-cut temple at Abu Simbel. The temple was guarded by four gigantic statues of the Pharaoh (see right), and was designed so that twice a year the rising sun would reach the innermost part and illuminate the statues of the gods.

The Hypostyle Hall at Karnak

An example of a painted column

An elaborate pendant hung on a string of beads is called a pectoral. The Scarab Pectoral (above) was found amongst the treasures of Tutankhamun's tomb.
The boy-king's gold death mask (left) was inlaid with semi-precious stones, such as lapis lazuli.

DATECHART

c.1552-1085 BC
The New Kingdom (Dynasties XVIII-XX)
c.1552-1305 BC
Dynasty XVIII
c.1492-1479 BC
Reign of Tuthmosis II
c.1473-1458 BC
Reign of Queen Hatshepsut. Expedition to Punt.
c.1479-1425 BC
Reign of Tuthmosis III. The Egyptian Empire reaches its greatest extent.
c.1364-1347 BC
Reign of Akhenaten (Amenhotep IV)
c.1347-1337 BC
Reign of Tutankhamun
c.1305-1186 BC
Dynasty XIX
c.1289-1224 BC
Reign of Ramesses II
c.1184-1153 BC
Reign of Ramesses III (Dynasty XX)
c.1085-664 BC The Third Intermediate Period

Akhenaten

Abu Simbel

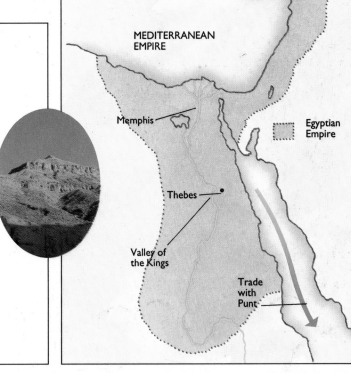

MEDITERRANEAN EMPIRE

Memphis

Egyptian Empire

Thebes

Valley of the Kings

Trade with Punt

THE GODS OF EGYPT

The Ancient Egyptians believed in a large number of gods and goddesses who controlled all aspects of nature and daily life. During the Old and Middle Kingdoms the main god was the Sun god, Re; during the New Kingdom, the King of gods was Amun-Re. The main goddess was Isis, the protector of all. Certain gods were special to cities or towns. For example, Ptah was the creator god of Memphis. Many of the gods and goddesses were shown with animal heads. These represented a particular quality and made the deities easier to recognise.

Many of the gods and goddesses were closely related. Re's son, Shu, was god of the air and father of the sky goddess, Nut. She was married to her brother, Geb, the god of the earth. Osiris, the Ruler of the Dead, was the son of Nut and Geb. His wife was his sister, Isis, the mother goddess. Their son was Horus, the falcon-headed god. The main gods and goddesses are shown below.

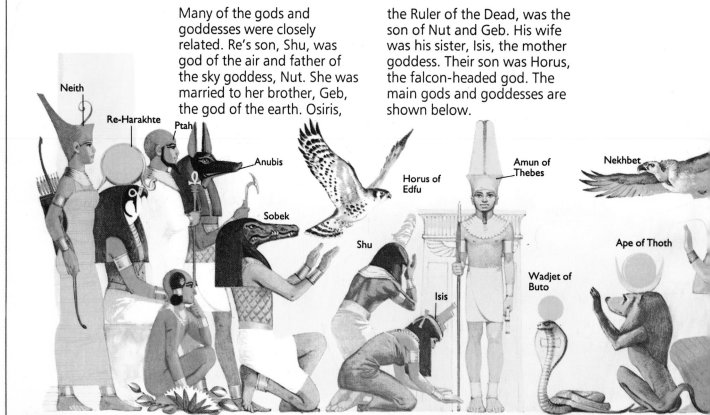

Neith
Re-Harakhte
Ptah
Anubis
Sobek
Shu
Horus of Edfu
Isis
Amun of Thebes
Wadjet of Buto
Nekhbet
Ape of Thoth

Akhenaten
Amenhotep IV ruled Ancient Egypt from about 1364 to 1347 BC. He was married to Queen Nefertiti. Amenhotep tried to reform the religion of Ancient Egypt and is thought to be the first person to have worshipped one god, rather than several deities. This was the sun god, Aten. In honour of his god, the king changed his name to Akhenaten. However, Akhenaten upset many Egyptians by forbidding them to worship the old gods. They were later restored by his successor, Tutankhamun.

Akhenaten

Temple worship

Ordinary people worshipped the gods at home. The temples were reserved for the priests, priestesses and the chief priest, the Pharaoh himself. A temple was seen as the god's home on Earth. The god's statue was kept in a shrine deep inside the temple complex. Each day, the priests brought the statue out, cleaned and dressed it and offered it food and drink. The priestesses said prayers and sang sacred hymns.

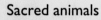

Khnum

Thoth

Khonsu

Mestert

Osiris

Sekhmet

Hathor with son, Ihy

Lucky charms

Jewellery was worn by everybody in Ancient Egypt. The pattern on many pieces contained special symbols which were thought to protect the wearer. These were also worn as amulets or charms. Among the luckiest amulets were the ankh, the symbol of life, and the udjat eye. The eye was said to protect everything behind it.

Funerary amulets

Sacred animals

The Ancient Egyptians believed that animals such as cats and bulls, and birds such as ibises were special to certain gods and goddesses. One chosen animal was kept in the temple where, it was believed, the spirit of the deity passed into it at certain times. The Egyptians worshipped this divine spirit that came to Earth temporarily. Such animals were considered to be the deity's chosen vessel, and were therefore treated with the utmost respect. During the Late Period, anyone who killed a cat was sentenced to death. Sacred animals were often mummified.

Sacred scarab amulets

Cats often wore a gold ring to show they were sacred.

SOCIAL STRUCTURE

Ancient Egyptian society was headed by the Pharaoh. Below him came the royal family and members of the upper classes, including noblemen and landowners, government officials, high-ranking army officials and priests. Merchants, scribes, craftsmen, soldiers and sailors made up the middle class. The largest class was the lower class. It consisted of peasants and farmers. Below them came the slaves, although they too had legal rights. People could move into a higher class if they married well or got a better job.

Pharaoh

The Ancient Egyptians wore skirts, dresses and robes made of white linen. Wealthier people also wore headdresses and wigs.

Priest

The queen

Nobleman

Nobleman's wife

Bronze mirror

Eyeshadow palate

Jewellery box

Egyptian style

Both men and women wore make-up and jewellery in Ancient Egypt. To begin their toilet, Egyptians would wash with a special cleansing paste and water. They used eyeliner, called kohl, made from ground copper or iron ore and mixed with oil. Lips and cheeks were painted with red clay (ochre) mixed with water. They admired themselves in mirrors made of highly polished silver or copper. Henna was very popular amongst the Ancient Egyptians for dying hair, and was also used to redden palms and the soles of feet. Perfumes made from oils scented with cinnamon and myrrh were also widely available in Ancient Egypt.

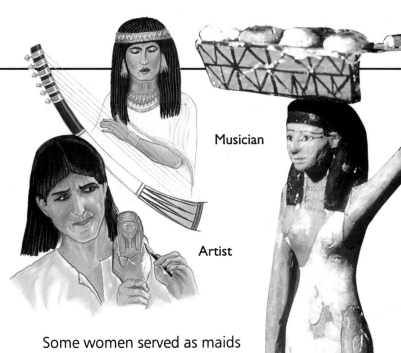

Musician

Artist

Some women served as maids to the wives of wealthy nobles or as nurses, gardeners, weavers and professional mourners. They were also employed as singers, dancers, acrobats and musicians. Wealthier women often became priestesses and even doctors. Women could own property, and run it either in their own right, or on behalf of their husband or sons. Daughters could inherit land if their parents had no sons. Women were not allowed to hold government positions, but they could conduct their own court cases and business deals.

Women in society
In most ancient societies, woman had very few rights but in Egypt they were greatly respected and had many rights and privileges (see left). In Egyptian art, women have pale skins, suggesting that they spent most of their time indoors. Men are usually portrayed as darker-skinned.

The statue shown left is of a servant girl carrying offerings.

Family life
Family life and children were very important to the Ancient Egyptians. They adopted children if they could not have their own. The father was the head of the family, with his eldest son as his heir. Most sons followed in their father's profession. Girls learnt how to cook, sew and look after the household.

The engraving, right, depicts Nebamun and his wife and daughter hunting in the marshes. The hieroglyphic text refers to "having pleasure, [and] seeing good things..."

THE FARMER'S YEAR

Farming was the mainstay of Egypt's economy and the source of its great prosperity. Most people worked as farmers on large estates. The fertile soil deposited by the Nile each year enabled huge numbers of crops to be grown. The farmers paid the landowner part of their crops. The landowners also had to give larger amounts of farm produce as taxes to the King. The crops grown were wheat and barley to make bread and beer, flax to make linen, dates and grapes to make wine and a large variety of fruit and vegetables.

Agricultural developments
Because Egypt was so hot and dry, irrigation was essential. Irrigation canals were dug from the River Nile and a device called a *shaduf*, used to raise the water to the fields. The *shaduf* consisted of a beam with a weight on one end and a bucket on the other. A man dipped the bucket into the river, let the weight pull it up, and poured the water into the canal. This device is still in use today.

A shaduf

The farmer's year was split into three seasons – the Inundation season (July to November), the Growing season (November to March) and the Harvest (March to July). No work could be done during the Inundation so many farmers worked on royal buildings (see pages 8/9).

When the floods went down, they ploughed the land and sowed the seed. In March, the taxmen decided how much produce to take in tax. The wheat could then be harvested.

Tooth trouble
Bread was one of the basic foods in the Egyptian diet. The grain for the bread was ground into flour between two stones. This was often done outdoors. Analysis of ancient loaves has shown it often contained pieces of grit, which may have blown in while the bread was being made. Some mummies have teeth worn down by chewing gritty bread.

Lavish feasts
Wealthy Egyptians enjoyed entertaining their friends with lavish banquets. The menu might include roast goose or exotic meats, cakes, figs and plenty of wine. Food was eaten with the fingers. Between courses, a servant brought a basin and jug of water for the diners to rinse their hands. Guests sat with cones of perfumed fat on their heads. When these melted in the heat, they helped to cool the guests' heads down.

Donkeys were used to carry the harvested wheat to the threshing floor. Cattle were driven across the wheat to separate the grain from the husk. The wheat was then tossed into the air, the husk allowed to blow away and the grain put into large baskets.

The calendar

As early as the Old Kingdom, the Ancient Egyptians had devised a 365-day calendar with twelve 30-day months and five additional days. The calendar was based on the flooding of the Nile and the appearance of the star, Sirius. Once a year, Sirius rises on the eastern horizon a couple of moments before dawn. The Egyptians calculated that the appearance of the star coincided with the annual flooding of the Nile. This date was therefore fixed as the beginning of their calendar year. The Egyptian calendar has enabled scholars to date much of the history of Egypt and the ancient world, and is the basis of the calendar we use today. Egyptian scholars also divided the day into 24 hours – the length of our modern day.

Grain was stored in large granaries until it was needed. Wheat was ground into flour and used to make bread; barley was made into beer. The Egyptians also grew onions, garlic, lettuces, beans, melons and figs. They raised cattle, sheep, pigs, ducks, geese and goats, and some kept bees for honey which was used for sweetening. The Nile provided plenty of fish and wild fowl. Whole meals were put into people's tombs for them to eat in the next world.

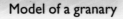

Model of a granary

The engraving left shows a scribe counting the geese and eggs, while the herdsmen bow before their master.

The engraving (right) shows fashionable ladies offering each other lotus blooms. Ladies were usually seated apart from the men at banquets.

EGYPTIANS AT HOME

Egyptian houses varied greatly in size and splendour depending on the wealth and status of their owners. Houses built in towns were crowded together along narrow streets, and were often several storeys high. Those who could afford it also had a villa in the countryside, with exotic gardens full of trees and flowers. Poorer families lived in just one room, which served as a living, dining and bedroom. Cooking was often done outside the house, to reduce the risk of fire in the tiny, cramped conditions. Richer households had several rooms, including separate servants' quarters.

Shrine

Garden

Central hall

Granary court

Kitchens

Servants' quarters

This is the country villa of a wealthy noble. At the front is a reception area where business was conducted. Behind that is a columned hall where guests were entertained. The family's private rooms, which included bedrooms and bathrooms, were at the back of the house. Behind them were the kitchen and even a grain silo, as each house stored grain to make its own bread and beer. There were also beautiful gardens, with a pool. It was kept well stocked with fish and lotus flowers. The whole villa was surrounded by a high wall.

Furniture
Egyptian houses were furnished with wooden chairs, beds, chests and tables. These might be carved from local sycamore fig wood. Colourful wall-hangings often adorned the walls. The king and nobles had furniture made of precious ebony or cedar wood, inlaid with gold or precious stones. Chairs were considered a sign of wealth and high social status. Oil lamps with flax wicks were used for lighting.

Building materials

Temples were meant to last for ever, and so were built out of stone. The first houses, however, were built of reeds. Later houses were all made of mud bricks, dried and hardened in the sun. The mud was mixed with grit and straw, shaped and left to dry. Mud plaster was also used to cover the floor. The finished house was coated with limestone plaster. Very few Ancient Egyptian houses have survived to the present day.

A model showing brickmakers

Flat roofs for cooking and storage

Cooking was done in a domed oven

The houses of poor Egyptians were much smaller and less luxurious than the villa. They had very little furniture, and were often cramped. On hot nights, people slept on the roof where it was cooler. Models of poorer houses have been found in tombs. They show houses with low, arched doorways and small courtyards. Windows were often small and placed near the ceiling, to avoid the intense sunlight.

Fun and games

Egyptian children loved toys and games like knucklebones and leapfrog. They played with dolls, balls and spinning tops and wooden animals. The jaw of the wooden lion shown left snaps shut when the string is jerked. One of the most popular board games was called *senet* (shown below). The aim of the game was to reach the kingdom of Osiris, overcoming various evils and obstacles on the way. *Senet* was played with counters, rather like backgammon. Four *senet* boards were found buried with King Tutankhamun.

Wooden lion

The magnificent throne of Tutankhamun (left)

A folding stool (below)

23

BURIAL CUSTOMS

The Ancient Egyptians were firm believers in life after death. They went to great lengths to prepare themselves for death, burial and the life to come. They believed that a dead person's soul travelled into an underworld, called Duat. Here it had to pass through many trials and ordeals, before it could reach the next world, the Kingdom of the West. There, it could lead a life very like the one it had known in Egypt, but free from trouble. The Ancient Egyptians believed that a person had three souls – the *ka*, the *ba* and the *akh*. They could only survive in the next world if the body was preserved and not left to rot. This led to bodies being mummified.

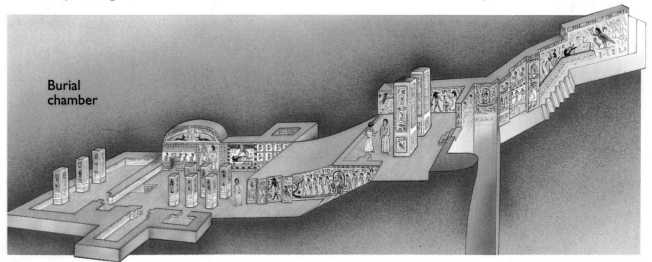

Burial chamber

The tombs of the New Kingdom kings were cut deep into the rocks of a valley at Thebes. They consist of a central tunnel with rooms off, leading to the burial chamber (see above). Many Middle Kingdom tombs contain tomb models. Non-royal tombs from all periods show activities from everyday life, such as grinding corn or ploughing the fields. Hundreds of magical statues of servants, called *shabti*, have been found in the tombs of wealthy Egyptians. If Osiris ordered you to work in the fields or do some other menial task in the underworld, you could get the *shabti* to do it for you.

Model of woman grinding corn

The Egyptians filled their tombs with objects which they might need in the afterlife. These included clothes, food and furniture. Tomb walls were painted with scenes from daily life. Osiris, the Ruler of the Dead, was supposed to bring these to life.

Shabti figure of Amenhotep II

Poor burials
Very few Egyptians could afford splendid tombs or grand coffins. Poor people were often buried in simple holes in the hot sand or in a small tomb cut into the ground. However, all Egyptians, whether rich or poor, believed that if they had led a good, virtuous life, Osiris would reward them with a happy eternal life.

Wooden model of a funerary boat

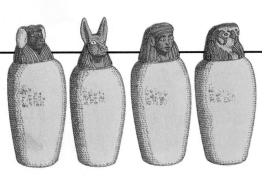

Canopic
jars

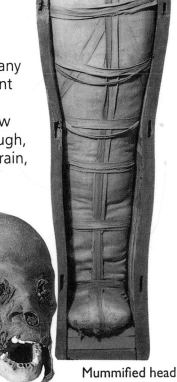

Mummification

Bodies were mummified to stop them from
rotting. The process was so successful that many
have survived, remarkably intact, to the present
day. There were different degrees of
mummification, depending on how
rich a person was. In general, though,
the first step was to remove the brain,
liver, lungs and intestines. These
were stored in special jars, called
canopic jars (shown above).
The heart was left in place
(see below). Then the body was
packed in crystals of natron salt to
dry it out. The body was padded
with cloth to make it look fleshier,
then oiled and wrapped in strips of
linen before being placed in its coffin.
The process took about 70 days.

Mummified head

Funerary texts

Passages of prayers, spells and hymns
were carved on tomb walls. These
were intended to guide the dead person
through the afterlife, to protect them from evil
and provide for their future needs. The texts
were later written down on papyrus scrolls and
became known as The Book of the Dead. The
texts and spells were often accompanied by
colourful illustrations, such as the one shown
below.

In the Judgement Hall, the dead
person would stand trial before the
god, Osiris. The engraving, right,
shows Anubis (the figure on the left
with the head of a jackal) preparing
to weigh the dead person's heart
against a feather, the symbol of
truth. If he had led a sinful life, his
heart would tip the scales and he
would be punished. If he had led a
good life, his heart and the feather
would balance and he could go on
to join his ancestors. The verdict is
recorded by Thoth, god of wisdom.

FOREIGN PHARAOHS

The end of Dynasty XX signalled the start of Egypt's gradual decline. Egypt was ruled by a series of foreign kings – from Libya, Nubia and Assyria. In 664 BC, Egyptian kings regained power to form Dynasty XXVI. In 525 BC, however, Egypt was conquered by the Persians who ruled until 404 BC. A brief period of Egyptian rule followed but the Persians returned in 341 BC. Alexander the Great defeated the Persians and made Egypt part of his empire. In 30 BC, Egypt finally fell to the Romans.

Alexander the Great, King of Macedonia and leader of the Greeks, conquered the Persians and arrived in Egypt in 332 BC. He was hailed as a saviour by the Egyptians, who hated their tyrannical Persian rulers. However, when Alexander died in 323 BC, his empire was divided up. His general, Ptolemy, took control of Egypt, and in about 305 BC, he declared himself King of Egypt. He began the Ptolemaic Dynasty, which was to rule Egypt for the next 250 years. Under the early Ptolemies, Egyptian trade and culture flourished. However, by the 2nd century BC, frequent power struggles within the family threatened the royal authority. Many Ptolemaic rulers seized or retained the throne by murdering close relatives who had a claim to it. Unrest grew between the native Egyptians and their Greek rulers.

The Pharos
of Alexandria

Alexander
the Great

Port building

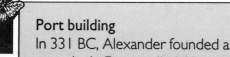

In 331 BC, Alexander founded a new city in Egypt, called Alexandria, on the Mediterranean coast. It had two fine harbours and was designed to become a major port. Under Ptolemy, it became Egypt's capital and quickly established itself as a great centre of culture and learning. Some of the greatest scholars came to study at its Museum and library. The city is also famous for its lighthouse – the Pharos of Alexandria, shown above – one of Seven Wonders of the World. The Pharos was built in about 270 BC, and was the world's first lighthouse. It stood about 122 metres high, and was built of white marble. Its light came from a wood-burning fire situated in the top of the lighthouse. The Pharos lighthouse was destroyed by an earthquake in AD 1375.

Antony and Cleopatra

Cleopatra VII was the last of the Ptolemaic rulers. With her Roman husband, Mark Antony, she tried to keep Egypt powerful. In 31 BC, however, Antony and Cleopatra were defeated by the Romans at the Battle of Actium. They committed suicide and Egypt became part of the Roman Empire. Antony and Cleopatra have inspired many writers and poets, such as Shakespeare.

The Late Period of Egyptian history lasted from about 664-332 BC. Egypt recovered some of its power under the so-called Saite kings of Dynasty XXVI. But in 525 BC, King Psamtek III was defeated by the Persian ruler, Cambyses and Egypt became part of the huge Persian empire.

Influence on art

Under Alexander and the Ptolemies, Greek art and culture spread to Egypt and began to influence the age-old traditions and conventions of Egyptian art and sculpture. Many of the reliefs carved into the walls of temples during this period show a mixture of Greek and Egyptian styles.

This king's head was carved during the Ptolemaic period

DATECHART

c.1069-664 BC
The Third Intermediate Period (Dynasties XXI-XXV)
c.728-664 BC
Nubian kings rule (Dynasty XXV)
c.664-332 BC
The Late Period (Dynasty XXVI–XXX)
c.664-525 BC
Rule of the Saite kings (Dynasty XXVI)
c.525 BC
The Persians invade Egypt
c.404-341 BC
Egypt regains its independence under Dynasties XXVIII, XXIX and XXX
c.341-332 BC
The Persians return and rule Egypt
332 BC Alexander the Great defeats the Persians and conquers Egypt
323 BC
Death of Alexander
323-30 BC
The Ptolemies rule Egypt
31 BC
Mark Antony and Cleopatra defeated by the Roman ruler, Octavian, at the Battle of Actium
30 BC
Suicide of Mark Antony and Cleopatra. Egypt becomes part of the Roman Empire.
AD324
Egypt is converted to Christianity
AD639-642
The Arabs conquer Egypt and convert many to Islam

Alexandria

Ptolemaic Empire at its height

THE EGYPTIAN LEGACY

Since Champollion unlocked the secrets of the Rosetta Stone in 1822, people have marvelled at the skills and knowledge of the Ancient Egyptians. They built great cities and monuments – those still standing attract millions of visitors each year. They created exquisite works of art and sculpture. They produced advanced studies of astronomy, mathematics, geography and medicine. Egyptian doctors were the first to make a scientific study of the human body. The civilisation of Ancient Egypt died out more than 2,000 years ago, but its fascination continues – and there is still plenty left to discover.

The Nile today

The Nile is the main transport route of modern Egypt, as it was in the past. Boats called *feluccas* and *dhows* carry goods and passengers. But the river does not flood any more. The Aswan High Dam was built between 1960-1970 to control the waters of the Nile. Water for irrigation and hydroelectric power now collects in the man-made Lake Nasser behind the dam. However, the dam also traps a lot of soil on the bed of Lake Nasser. The rich, silty soil that once made the farmland bordering the Nile so fertile, is no longer deposited. As a result, the Nile has begun to recede in some places.

Thousands of people visit Egypt each year, drawn by the grandeur of this ancient civilisation.

Some Egyptian monuments, such as the carved stone pillar, called an obelisk, shown above left, were removed from Egypt during the last century. They can now be found in cities throughout the world. The pyramids at Giza (above), however, could not be moved, and stand as monuments to a great civilisation. Ancient Egyptian influence can also be detected in some modern architecture, such as churches, bridges, and even cemeteries. The building shown right in Miami, Florida, reveals the Egyptian influence on the Art Deco movement of the 1920s. Art Deco favours strong geometric shapes and smooth lines.

Agriculture today

Up until the 1800s, Egyptian farmers relied upon the yearly Inundation to irrigate their fields and renew the layer of topsoil. Much of Egypt's land is still divided into small fields, surrounded by irrigation ditches (see right), although today, a system has been introduced which allows the land to be irrigated all year round. Dams, canals and reservoirs were built to trap the water from the Nile. This system was completed when the Aswan Dam was opened in 1968 (see left). Today, cotton is Egypt's most valuable cash crop, and dates, grown mainly in the desert oases, are perhaps the best known. Maize, oranges, potatoes, rice, sugar cane and tomatoes are also grown.

The *shaduf* used in Ancient Egypt (see page 20) can still be found today in some parts of Egypt (right). However, many are now being replaced with electrically driven pumps.

Family planning
Egyptian knowledge of anatomy stemmed from the practice of mummification. This knowledge later influenced Greek medicine. The Ancient Egyptians also practised contraception (birth control), to limit the size of their families. One method involved the use of honey as a barrier. A far less sweet solution was to use a ball of dung!

c.**5000-3100 BC** Predynastic Period. Small communities of farmers united to form two kingdoms – Upper and Lower Egypt. The King of Upper Egypt wore the White Crown and his capital was at Hierakonopolis. The King of Lower Egypt wore the Red Crown. His capital was at Buto.

c.**3100-2686** Archaic Period (Dynasties I-II). Upper and Lower Egypt united by Menes, who was the first Pharaoh. He built a new capital at Memphis. Royal tombs built near Abydos and Saqqara.

c.**2686-2150** The Old Kingdom (Dynasties III-VI). One of the greatest periods of Egyptian history. The pyramid age.

2686-2613 Reign of King Zoser

2613-2505 Reigns of Pharaohs Khufu, Khafre and Menkaure. Great Pyramids and Sphinx built at Giza.

c.**2150-2040** First Intermediate Period (Dynasties VII-X). Collapse of kings' rule; social and political chaos, wars and famine.

c.**2040-1640** The Middle Kingdom (Dynasties XI-XIII). Egypt reunited by a Prince of Thebes (modern Luxor).

c.**1640-1552** Second Intermediate Period (Dynasties XIV-XVII). Another period of chaos. Invasion by foreigners called Hyksos, who ruled northern Egypt.

c.**1552-1085** The New Kingdom (Dynasties XVIII-XX). Hyksos driven out by Pharaoh Ahmose I. Empire expanded by Tuthmosis III. Other significant rulers include Hatshepsut, Amenhotep IV (Akhenaton), Tutankhamun, Haremhab and Ramesses II and III. Kings buried in rock-cut tombs in the Valley of the Kings at Thebes.

c.**1085-664 BC** Third Intermediate Period

 8000BC

First hieroglyphs (picture writing) in Egypt c.3500BC

Old Kingdom in Egypt 2686-2150 BC.

Pyramids built in Egypt during Old Kingdom

Egyptian Middle Kingdom 2040-1640 BC

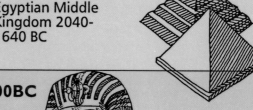

2000BC

Tutankhamun – the boy Pharaoh 1347-1337 BC

New Kingdom in Egypt 1552-1085 BC

Romulus and Remus found the city of Rome 753 BC

500BC

Roman Empire c.27 BC-c.AD 476

Julius Caesar murdered 44 BC

Fall of the Roman Empire AD 476

Viking raids on Britain and France AD 793-1000

AD1000

First Crusade to recapture Holy Land from Muslims AD1096

First mechanical clock developed AD 1380

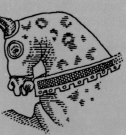

The Aztec Empire in Central America AD 1300-1521

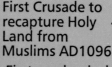

AD 1350-1532 Growth of the Inca Empire in South America

8000-5650 BC
First cities – Jericho and
Catal Hüyük

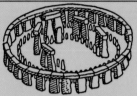

3500-3000 BC
Wheel invented
by the Sumerians

2500-1500 BC
Rise of the Indus
Valley civilisation

Early Minoan period in
Crete begins c.2500 BC

Stonehenge
completed in
England c.1500 BC

The destruction of
Knossos in Crete.
End of the Minoan
period c.1200 BC

c.500 BC
Life of
Gautama
the
Buddha

c.1400-1027 BC
Shang dynasty in China.

Birth of Confucius c. 551

The Golden Age of
Greece 478-405 BC

Alexander the Great
conquers Persia, Syria
and Egypt 332 BC

The first Empire in China
221 BC-AD 618

The Great Wall in China
completed in 214 BC.

Samurai warriors of Japan
from AD 1100-1850

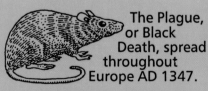

The Plague,
or Black
Death, spread
throughout
Europe AD 1347.

First mechanical printing
press developed by
Gutenberg in
Germany in
AD 1455.

Christopher Columbus sets
sail for the West Indies and
became the first European
to discover America.

GLOSSARY

Ankh A lucky amulet which was the symbol of life.

Cataract A place where the River Nile was blocked by rocks.

Deben Copper weights used in trade, instead of money.

Duat The Ancient Egyptian underworld.

Dynasty A line of kings from the same family. The dynasties of Ancient Egypt run from I to XXX.

Hieroglyphics The Ancient Egyptian system of picture writing.

Hyksos A group of people from Asia who invaded Ancient Egypt in about 1670 BC.

Inundation The annual flooding of the River Nile which provided farmers with fertile, silty soil.

Mummy The preserved body of an Ancient Egyptian which had been treated with oils and bound in linen strips.

Nome An administrative district of Ancient Egypt, governed on behalf of the king by a nomarch.

Papyrus A material for writing on, made out of reeds.

Pharaoh The name given to the King of Egypt after about 1554 BC. The title means "great house".

Pyramid A tomb built for an Ancient Egyptian king. The pyramids rank amongst the greatest of all engineering feats.

Shaduf A device used by farmers in Ancient Egypt for raising water from the Nile up to their fields. It is still in use today.

INDEX

Abu Simbel 15
Akhenaten 16
Alexander the Great 26, 27
Alexandria 26
amulets 17
Antony and Cleopatra 27
armour and weapons 11
army 11
art and sculpture 11, 15, 27, 28
Aswan High Dam 28, 29
Aztec pyramids 9

birth control 29
boats 7, 14
building materials 8, 9, 23
burial customs 8, 24-5

calendar 21
children 19, 23
cosmetics 18
costume 18
cultural legacy 5, 28

date charts 6, 10, 15, 27, 30-1
desert areas 5

family life 19
farming 5, 20-1, 29
food 20, 21
furnishings 22

games 23
Giza 6, 7, 8, 28
gods and goddesses 6, 16-17, 24
government 7

Great Pyramid of Giza 8

Hatshepsut 14
hieroglyphics 12, 13
houses 22, 23

Inundation 5, 9, 20, 29
irrigation 5, 20, 29

jewellery 17, 18
Joseph and his Amazing Technicolour Dreamcoat 5

Karnak 15
kings 6-7, 8

language 12
life after death 24, 25
Lower Egypt 4, 5

Memphis 4, 16
Middle Kingdom 10-11, 16
modern Egypt 28-9
mummification 17, 24, 25

natural resources 5
New Kingdom 14-15, 16
Nile 4, 5, 20, 21, 28
Nubia 6, 7, 10

oases 5
obelisks 28
Old Kingdom 6-7, 16
Osiris 16, 24, 25

papyrus 13
pectorals 15
Persian Empire 26, 27

Pharaohs 6, 11, 17, 18
Pharos of Alexander 26
Ptolemies 26, 27
pyramids 6, 7, 8-9, 28

Ramesses II 14, 15
religious worship 16-17
Roman Empire 27
Rosetta Stone 12, 13

sacred animals 17
science and medicine 28, 29
scribes 12
scripts 13
Sea Peoples 14
shaduf 20, 29
slaves 18
social system 18-19
soldiers 11
sphinxes 7

taxation 7, 20
temples 15, 17, 23
The Book of the Dead 25
tombs 7, 8-9, 14, 24
trade 5, 6, 7, 10
Tutankhamun 14, 15, 16, 23

Upper Egypt 4, 5

villas 22
viziers 7

wadis 5
women in society 19, 21
writing 12-13

Photographic Credits:

The majority of pictures were reproduced by Courtesy of the Trustees of the British Museum apart from the following images. Front cover right: Roger Vlitos; back cover left, title page,4, 5, top, 6 top, 6-7, 9, 12 top, 14 top, 14-15, 15 right, 16 top, 28 top & bottom & 29 top: Dr Anne Millard; 14 bottom: Spectrum Colour Library; 15 left & 23 bottom left: Robert Harding Picture Library; 28-29: Charles de Vere; 29 middle: Hutchinson Library; 29 bottom Frank Spooner Pictures.